THE FUTURE IS FEMALE

ALTERNATOR BOOKS™

Changemakers in

BUSINESS

Women Leading the Way

DR. ARTIKA R. TYNER

T0018881

Lerner Publications ◆ Minneapolis

This book is dedicated to my Grandma Nellie who taught me the importance of entrepreneurship and service in the community.

Lerner Publications Company
An imprint of Lerner Publishing Group, Inc.
241 First Avenue North
Minneapolis, MN 55401 USA

For reading levels and more information, look up this title at www.lernerbooks.com.

Main body text set in Aptifer Sans LT Pro Medium.
Typeface provided by Linotype AG.

Editor: Brianna Kaiser **Designer:** Athena Currier **Photo Editor:** Nicole Berglund
Lerner team: Martha Kranes

Library of Congress Cataloging-in-Publication Data

Names: Tyner, Artika R., author.
Title: Changemakers in business : women leading the way / Dr. Artika R. Tyner.
Description: Minneapolis : Lerner Publications, [2024] | Series: The future is female |
    Includes bibliographical references and index. | Audience: Ages 8–12 | Audience:
    Grades 4–6 | Summary: "Many women are leading the way in business, but do you
    know who they are? Readers will discover the female founders and CEOs of largely
    successful companies, self-made billionaires, and more"— Provided by publisher.
Identifiers: LCCN 2023010615 (print) | LCCN 2023010616
    (ebook) | ISBN 9798765608845 (hardback) | ISBN 9798765624982 (paperback) |
    ISBN 9798765618264 (epub)
Subjects: LCSH: Businesswomen—Juvenile literature. | Women chief executive
    officers—Juvenile literature. | Success in business—Juvenile literature. |
    Entrepreneurship—Juvenile literature. | BISAC: JUVENILE NONFICTION / Biography
    & Autobiography / Women
Classification: LCC HD6053 .T96 2024 (print) | LCC HD6053 (ebook) |
    DDC 331,4/8165484—dc23/eng/20230601

LC record available at https://lccn.loc.gov/2023010615
LC ebook record available at https://lccn.loc.gov/2023010616

Manufactured in the United States of America
1-1009546-51562-6/21/2023

Table of Contents

First Black Female Billionaire

After not seeing herself or her community represented on television, Sheila Johnson decided to take action. She wanted to see talented Black actors, musicians, and artists featured on television. So in 1980, Johnson and her then-husband, Robert Johnson, created Black Entertainment Television (BET).

With hard work, Sheila Johnson became the first Black female billionaire. She was named the 2022 chief executive officer (CEO) of the year by the *Washington Business Journal*.

Sheila Johnson receives the 2019 W. E. B. Du Bois Medal for her contribution to Black culture.

This book highlights women such as Johnson who have made great changes in business. Not every female business leader is featured in this book. But you'll learn about many powerful women who are creating new pathways for other women to lead and succeed in business.

CHAPTER 1

Entrepreneurs Leading the Way

Entrepreneurs organize and run a business.
They see a problem and create a solution. They bring people together to develop new ideas, create jobs, and serve in their communities.

Creating Jobs

Two years after moving to California, Janice Bryant Howroyd struggled to find a job. She knew others faced similar challenges and made a plan. In 1978 Howroyd founded ActOne Group to support people in finding jobs and building

Janice Bryant Howroyd speaking at a 2013 BET event

careers. The company operates in thirty-three countries around the world and serves seventeen thousand people.

Howroyd is worth over $600 million. She is the first Black woman in the US to start and own a billion-dollar company. By creating jobs and opportunities for thousands of people, she makes a big impact on her community.

BEAUTY AND SUPPORT

Barbadian singer Rihanna (*below*) is the youngest self-made female billionaire in the US. Her makeup company, Fenty Beauty, is one of the reasons for this success. Rihanna uses her money to support others in need. In 2012 she founded the Clara Lionel Foundation. Named after her grandparents, it supports actions to address climate change in the US and the Caribbean.

Making Natural Products

In 2008 actor Jessica Alba got a rash after using a detergent to wash her baby's clothing. She decided to make products that were not harmful so she could protect her family. This led Alba to cofound the Honest Company.

The company makes clean and natural products—products that don't use harmful ingredients—for everyone. The products include diapers, detergents, skin care items, and hair care items. As of 2023, the company has an estimated value of over $1 billion.

Jessica Alba promotes the Honest Company in 2016.

Hijabs for Health Care

Hilal Ibrahim is a designer and founder of Henna and Hijabs, a company that makes hijabs. These traditional head coverings are worn by some Muslim women for a variety of reasons, such as religious beliefs. The company designed the first

MAKEUP AND HEALTH

Singer and actor Selena Gomez (*below*) founded the makeup company Rare Beauty in 2019. Gomez uses the business to spread awareness of mental health—the health of a person's mind and emotions.

> "I tell every young woman and girl that I meet to believe in herself and to know that whatever idea you have in mind, whatever dream that you have, whatever goal that you have, if there's something that you're thinking of or dreaming or planning to do, you can do it."
>
> —HILAL IBRAHIM, 2021

hijabs that women working in health care could wear. These hijabs were made with a stretchy material that wouldn't slip. They also had slits at the ears so women wouldn't have to remove the hijab while using stethoscopes.

When the disease COVID-19 spread in 2020, Henna and Hijabs donated over eight hundred hijabs to women working in health care in Minnesota. In 2021 the company partnered with a chain of stores to sell their hijabs.

In 2022 Hilal Ibrahim attends an event in New York City for business leaders.

CHAPTER 2

Tackling Business and Finance

Business leadership roles can enable people to make a difference. Business leaders can have a positive impact on and educate others.

A Global Business

Sonia Cheng is a leader in the hotel business. After studying math at Harvard, she worked in real estate. She learned how small companies work and grow into larger companies. This helped her later take on her family businesses.

Cheng's family has built successful jewelry and real estate businesses. This includes Rosewood Hotel Group, which owns hotels around the world. In 2011 Cheng became the CEO of Rosewood Hotel Group at thirty years old. She works on improving the business to reach more people.

Sonia Cheng at the opening of a Rosewood Hotel in 2013

Saving for Futures

Each year, *Fortune* magazine ranks the five hundred largest US companies by the amount of money they take in. In 2021 Thasunda Brown Duckett became the fourth Black woman to lead a *Fortune* 500 company.

Duckett is the president and CEO of Teachers Insurance and Annuity Association of America (TIAA). The company works with people on their retirement plans. Duckett helps people save for their futures. This is because her father, Otis Brown, worked hard for many years but still did not have enough money to save for retirement.

Thasunda Brown Duckett receives a BET Award in 2023.

CULTURE THROUGH FASHION

Bethany Yellowtail is an award-winning fashion designer and the founder and CEO of the fashion brand B.Yellowtail. A member of the Northern Cheyenne Nation, Yellowtail started her brand in 2015 after not seeing her culture in the fashion world. Yellowtail uses fashion to advocate for the rights of women and girls.

Bethany Yellowtail attends the 2022 Green Carpet Fashion Awards.

Duckett created the Otis and Rosie Brown Foundation in honor of her parents. It celebrates leaders who are having a positive impact on their community. It also provides scholarships for students who are making a difference.

Tiffany Aliche presenting one of her books at a 2019 conference

Teaching Finances

Tiffany Aliche was a preschool teacher with $300,000 in debt. But she paid off her debt and started a company to teach others how to make better money decisions. Through her company, she has helped over two million women save more money and pay off their debts.

Aliche also teaches youth how to better handle their money. She helped write a bill, or a proposed law, that says middle school students need to learn about finances. This bill later became a law. She also wrote a children's book, *Happy Birthday Mali More*, to help young children learn about what matters to them.

CHAPTER 3

Making Change through Food

Women are creating new paths in business through food. They are introducing more healthful food options and restaurants, and celebrating cultures.

A Vegan Diet

After having health challenges, Tabitha Brown became a vegan. She doesn't eat foods that come from animals. She shared this journey and vegan recipes on social media and connected with over twelve million people.

In addition to making healthful foods, she created the vegan hair care brand Donna's Recipe. All the products are made with vegan ingredients. She wrote about stories from her life in the best-selling book *Feeding the Soul (Because It's My Business)* and also wrote the vegan cookbook *Cooking from the Spirit.*

Tabitha Brown attends a red carpet event in 2022.

BEVERAGE BIZ

Singer and songwriter Beyoncé (*below*) is a successful businessperson who invested in WTRMLN WTR. The company takes unused watermelons to make drinks with natural ingredients and reduce food waste.

The Award-Winning Chef

Christine Ha is an award-winning chef. She was the first blind chef to appear on the cooking competition show *MasterChef*. Her tasty dishes and cooking skills helped her to win the competition.

She has also launched two Vietnamese restaurants, the Blind Goat and Xin Chào, in Houston, Texas. Both restaurants were finalists for awards by the James Beard Foundation.

Christine Ha is a successful chef.

Left to right: Gordon Ramsay speaks with Ha and other *MasterChef* winners Luca Manfé and Courtney Lapresi on an epsiode of the show.

The foundation awards chefs that have made great achievements. Ha also advocates for people with disabilities.

Family Roots

Padma Lakshmi has worked many years in the food business. She was a judge on the cooking competition show *Top Chef* and is the host of *Taste the Nation with Padma Lakshmi*. In the show, she travels across the US and looks at diverse cultures

Padma Lakshmi appears on *The Late Show with Stephen Colbert* in 2021.

through food. Her passion for cooking and food was inspired by her family's culture.

Lakshmi wrote the children's book *Tomatoes for Neela* in 2021. It celebrates the women in her family and the lessons Lakshmi learned from them about cooking fresh fruits and vegetables. She has partnered with businesses for many projects, including for a collection of cooking products.

CHAPTER 4

Breaking Out in Technology

Technology is changing fast. Women use new technology to build businesses and shape ideas.

Building the Online Future

Sheryl Sandberg was an early leader at the technology company Google. In the early 2000s, she led a team in the advertising department. Her team put advertisements—notices that make people aware of a product or service—online and helped Google grow into a key search engine.

> **"So please ask yourself. What would I do if I weren't afraid? And then go do it."**
>
> —SHERYL SANDBERG, IN HER BOOK
> *LEAN IN: WOMEN, WORK, AND THE WILL TO LEAD*

From 2008 to 2022, she worked as the CEO of Facebook. She also wrote the 2013 book *Lean In: Women, Work, and the Will to Lead*. Throughout her career, Sandberg has supported gender and women's rights.

Sheryl Sandberg gives a speech about Facebook in 2017.

Judy Faulkner presenting at an event in 2019

Technology in Health Care

Computer programmer Judy Faulkner is the founder and CEO of Epic Systems. Her company creates programs to keep records of patients. Faulkner started the company in 1979 in her basement and had only two other part-time workers.

Epic Systems has since grown to serve over 250 million patients. Faulkner is a self-made billionaire. She uses her wealth to give back to others. In 2015 she signed the Giving Pledge to commit to giving much of her wealth to charities.

GETTING MENTORS

Stephanie Villanueva-Villar is the founder of Your Girl for Good. Your Girl for Good has mentorship programs and connects young girls of color with professional women in many careers.

Your Girl for Good has many mentorship programs in science and math.

Award-Winning Tools

After working as a lawyer and starting an Indian food brand, Priya Lakhani founded CENTURY Tech. She is the CEO of the award-winning business. CENTURY Tech makes artificial intelligence tools for schools and colleges. Artificial intelligence is the ability for computers to mimic human intelligence and make decisions. Lakhani hopes for more young women to take risks and start their own businesses.

Priya Lakhani founded CENTURY Tech in 2013.

CONCLUSION

Future Business Leaders

When women create businesses and succeed in their careers, they make it possible for other women to find success. They inspire young women to explore new career options and make positive change in their communities. You can be a leader too!

Many women around the world lead in business.

Glossary

advocate: to speak or act in favor of

chief executive officer (CEO): a person who leads a company and makes many company decisions

culture: the language, customs, art, and ideas of a group of people

debt: owing more money than a person can pay back

disability: a condition of the body or mind that makes it more difficult to do some activities

finance: the managing of money

found: to set up or create

foundation: a group that gives money to people in need

impact: having a strong effect on someone

mentorship: serving as a guide or teacher to another

retirement: when a person no longer works

scholarship: money given to students to help pay for their education

Source Notes

11   "How Young Women Are Leading Today: Hilal Ibrahim of Henna & Hijabs," YouTube video, 3:21, posted by WomensFoundationMN, September 27, 2021, https://www.youtube.com/watch?v=clpTBKZnWeQ&t=151s.

24   Sheryl Sandberg, *Lean In: Women, Work, and the Will to Lead* (New York: Knopf Doubleday, 2013), 26, e-book.

Learn More

Bolden, Tonya. *Changing the Equation: 50+ US Black Women in STEM*. New York: Abrams Books for Young Readers, 2020.

Britannica Kids: Rihanna
https://kids.britannica.com/students/article/Rihanna/570949

Dixon, Robert P., Jr. *Black Achievements in Business: Celebrating Oprah Winfrey, Moziah Bridges, and More*. Minneapolis: Lerner Publications, 2024.

Kiddle: Padma Lakshmi Facts for Kids
https://kids.kiddle.co/Padma_Lakshmi

Rebel Girls: "Awesome Women Entrepreneurs Kids Should Know"
https://www.rebelgirls.com/blog/awesome-women-entrepreneurs-every-enterprising-kid-should-know

Thimmesh, Catherine. *Girls Solve Everything: Stories of Women Entrepreneurs Building a Better World*. Boston: Houghton Mifflin Harcourt, 2022.

Tyner, Dr. Artika R. *Changemakers in Activism: Women Leading the Way*. Minneapolis: Lerner Publications, 2024.

Vital Voices: "13 Young Women Leaders You Need to Know"
https://www.vitalvoices.org/news-articles/news/13-young-women-leaders-you-need-to-know/

Index

Photo Acknowledgments

Image credits: AP Photo/Elise Amendola, p. 5; Chelsea Lauren/Stringer/Getty Images, p. 7; Dimitrios Kambouris/Getty Images, p. 8; Mat Hayward/Stringer/Getty Images, p. 9; AP Photo/Richard Shotwell/Invision, p. 10; Ilya S. Savenok/Stringer/Getty Images, p. 11; Chris Jackson/Getty Images, p. 13; Derek White/Stringer/Getty Images, p. 14; David M. Benett/Getty Images, p. 15; Marla Aufmuth/Getty Images, p. 16; AP Photo/Scott Kirkland/Sipa USA, p. 18; Christopher Polk/Getty Images, p. 19; South China Morning Post/Getty Images, p. 20; FOX/Getty Images, p. 21; CBS Photo Archive/Getty Images, p. 22; Vincent Isore/IP3/Getty Images, p. 24; AP Photo/Michelle Stocker/Wisconsin State Journal, p. 25; Kmatta/Getty Images, p. 26; Jamie Wiseman/ANL/Shutterstock, p. 27; Maskot/Getty Images, p. 29. Design elements: Old Man Stocker/Shutterstock; MPFphotography/Shutterstock; schab/Shutterstock.

Cover: Jerod Harris/Getty Images; Samir Hussein/Getty Images; Andrew H. Walker/AWNewYork/Shutterstock.